I0163688

The Elegant Nobody

The Elegant Nobody

Jagari Mukherjee

HAWAKAL

10

HAWAKAL

Published by Hawakal Publishers
185 Kali Temple Road, Nimta, Kolkata 700049
India

Email info@hawakal.com
Website www.hawakal.com

First edition January, 2020

Copyright © Jagari Mukherjee 2020

Cover design: Bitan Chakraborty

All rights reserved. No part of this publication may be reproduced or transmitted (other than for purposes of review/critique) in any form or by any means, electronic or mechanical, including photocopy, recording, or any information storage and retrieval system without prior permission in writing from the publisher or the copyright holder where applicable. The author asserts her moral right to be identified as the author of her work.

ISBN: 978-81-944212-4-5

Price: 300 INR | USD 11.99

Doubt thou the stars are fire;
Doubt the sun doth move;
Doubt truth to be a liar;
But never doubt I love.

William Shakespeare
(*Hamlet*, Act 2 Scene 2)

For
my Father,
who taught me the art of writing.

For Truth Can Be a Lie in Disguise

This volume of poems by Jagari Mukherjee starts with a four-line quotation from Act 2 Scene 2 of Shakespeare's *Hamlet*, where Hamlet is telling Ophelia not to doubt his love for her. Hamlet says, "Doubt truth to be a liar." What does it mean in isolation when a poet says it? Is a poet a liar because he/she doubts truth or are circumstances, life, beloveds liars? Or is it just that truth hides behind curtains? Does the poet now doubt truth because circumstances have lied to him or her? Perhaps, the poet doubts what appears as truth and invites the readers to do the same. Then, what does the imperative "doubt" imply when Hamlet speaks it no doubt with a pause? One can doubt the scientific facts that the stars are fire and that the sun moves. Hamlet tells Ophelia to doubt everything except his love. But why doubt everything? The third line gives the answer. One can doubt *because* truth can be a lie in disguise. But Shakespeare does not use the word "because" in the third line:

"Doubt truth to be a liar." The implied meaning though is "doubt because truth can be a liar" and the actor playing the character of Hamlet is to convey the implied meaning through a proper pause in his speech. It is the pause when the line is spoken that gives the implied meaning in the context. It is not "doubt that truth is a liar" but "doubt because truth is a liar." So whatever doubts that Ophelia's father and brother may have about Hamlet's love for her by evidence of what appears before them, she should not doubt his love for her because appearance can be deceptive. One who loves often gets deceived by what is not real and there is no foolproof evidence, circumstance, or situation that can vouch for true love. It is this lack of any external anchoring for true love that makes Ophelia commit suicide. Pressurized by the external world, the loadstone of her love in her heart becomes a millstone.

Many of Jagari Mukherjee's poems are heartbreak poems, speaking of deception in love—deceived sometimes by circumstances and sometimes by beloveds. But, like the elision of "because" by Shakespeare in the third line of the Hamlet quotation, there is a missing "because" in all her poems. And like the actor playing the character of Hamlet in the play, the readers of Jagari Mukherjee's poems have to pause for that implied imperative. No, one may not get to the truth by pausing, but there will appear an apparition of something that makes a poem amorphous and sublime. It is this nebulous and transcendent nature of Jagari Mukherjee's poems that make them so stunning and marvelous. In "Pulchritude" she discovers the very word that forms the title of the poem in a softcover thesaurus and turns it into a sensuous poem of a beautifully deceptive reality, an untruth, a make-belief world but so desirable. There is vulnerability is succumbing to such a phantasm. Beauty is not skin deep but all the appearance associated with beauty, the paraphernalia and the concoctions are so fleeting and yet deluding one to desire them. But why will anyone want to pursue or even purchase such a beauty? It is

because…

I am drawn out under the sky
where every season bears the scent
of cherry blossoms, and the
orange in the sun and
the soft charcoal of rain
are rare migratory birds.

This sky is so alluring but reality does not make every season bear the scent of cherry blossom. When Keats said "Beauty is truth," and if beauty is transient then truth too is ephemeral. All truths are lies in disguise because they are not eternal. A truth is a truth only for the moment of its existence. At a different moment of time that same truth can be a lie. It is a painful realization. How does Jagari Mukherjee come to such a realization? It is *because...* and here an apparition appears, an apparition that haunted Mary Lamb, Emily Dickinson, Virginia Woolf, Sylvia Plath and many others. When Jagari Mukherjee writes "Eros Thanatos," love and death coexist in her poem, love for life and death of love. Pause, for there is a missing "because."

Amit Shankar Saha
8th January, 2020
Calcutta

ACKNOWLEDGEMENTS

I thankfully acknowledge the editors of the following venues for being the first publisher of a few of my poems: *Bear River Review, The Pangolin Review, The Fox Poetry Box, The Metaworker, Kritya, Setu, Narrow Road, Ethos Literary Journal, Harbinger Asylum, IPPL journal, Better Than Starbucks, Cajun Mutt Press, Glomag, Yawp* and *The Conclusion Magazine.* Some of these poems were written on prompts of *Napowrimo/Glopowrimo 2019* by The Significant League and Celebrating World Poetry Writing Month With WE. I gratefully acknowledge Ampat Koshy and Smeetha Bhoumik for the opportunity.

A wonderful person I must acknowledge is Ashwini Bhasi. A poet par excellence, a single meeting with her changed my life and I decided to dedicate it to poetry.

I gratefully acknowledge Dustin Pickering for giving the collection a name, and for his blurb. Thanks to Vinita Agrawal and Nabina Das for their blurbs.

Humble gratitude to Tarfia Faizullah, my role model poet, my pole star, my workshop leader at Bear River Writers' Conference 2018.

My sister, Dishari Thornhill, has been my greatest supporter as well as a wonderful critic of my poetry. I owe it all to her.

I am grateful to my family and my friends who encouraged me during the process of writing. Special thanks are due to Amit Shankar Saha, who not only was kind enough to write the foreword to this book, but also made a home for me in the *Rhythm Divine Poets* family. My debt to him cannot be repaid in this lifetime. I thank Nikita Parik for being the coolest friend ever—a brilliant poet, an excellent editor, and my sweet soul-sister. Thanks to Sufia Khatoon for teaching me to "walk on stars" and to reach for them. I would also like to thank the members of my *Nawab Ka Darbar* group—Ria Banerjee, Anish Sinha and Ananya Bhattacharyya for appointing me their court poet and cheering me on in my poetic endeavors. I also thank Amrita Chatterjee, Aditi Chatterjee, Aditi Bhaduri, Moinak Dutta, Mallika Bhaumik, Linda Ashok, Lopamudra Banerjee, Aakriti Kuntal, Saima Afreen, Partha Roy, Sanjukta Dasgupta, Sharmila Ray, Anindita Bose, Smeetha Bhoumik, Gopal Lahiri, Amanita Sen, Madhabi Bhattacharya, Glory Sasikala, Amita Roy, Madhugiti Mitra, Saheli Mitra, Satbir Chadha,

Santosh Bakaya and Ruth Pal Chaudhuri for encouraging me during various stages of my journey. I cannot forget my friends who kept believing in me during several ups and downs: Ronita Sengupta, Sayantani Chakraborty, Alpana Phukan, and Anuja Kshatriya.

I thank my parents–my father who took me to readings and ensured that I never gave up, and my mother for her sheer patience and dedication. My extended family in the US, The Thornhills–Kyle, Darvis, Joanne, and Emily, deserve special mention. I would also like to express my gratitude to my poet friends in the US–Stephan Anstey, Scott Beal, Mike Zhai, Patrick W. Gibson, and Robb Astor. In fact, there are too many to be named, and I love them all to no end.

Last but not the least, much thanks to *Hawakal Publishers* for giving a home to my collection of poems.

CONTENTS

PULCHRITUDE*

Today, the green softcover thesaurus
gives me my favorite word.
'Pulchritude' enters my pulmonary artery
like a bright red ruby, turns
my blue veins into lapis lazuli.
Each exhalation has the fragrance
of flowers — now a daisy, next a periwinkle.
The synonyms are luminous
as if held under moonshine:
luscious, lovely, sultry, voluptuous
bearing the taste of
pomegranates and mulberries.
I am drawn out under the sky
where every season bears the scent
of cherry blossoms, and the
orange in the sun and
the soft charcoal of rain
are rare migratory birds.
Even the music of the first syllable
gathers the remainder
in a symphony.
Whatever it is, it is not skin deep.

*beauty

THE SUNLIT SENSUOUSNESS OF OUR DARKENED SOUL

give me the sun—
rust-orange silk
for the darkened soul—
or better still,
a scarlet satin veil...

first step, drape
next step, unclothe
and watch how the soul
glimmers, shimmers
belly-dancing before jeweled mirrors
dreaming of molding
my softness against your
rough tree-trunk
chafing silk-skin
tearing into satin

(where love is a sun
and every thought of you
makes me a sensuous dancer.)

SMOKE AND PAINT

Our loves, together, wafted like smoke
from a marijuana joint, astringent in
the inside of my chest, made breathing
a labor and every breath a child and
I kept looking only at your face...

We loved. No doubt.
The smoking, the smoldering, the welding of souls.
All in muggy weather.
You in a black buttoned shirt and I
under a black blanket and the rest of the world
in muted paints.

I remember not finding solace in a dream
where the only color came from
hard glittering butterflies on handmade paper.
I opened an envelope of blue boarding passes
and was borne through a crowded market
of cloudy hue.
All I thought of was black—and you.

PLAYMATE

As kids, you and I
loved red paper lanterns and exquisite Japanese dolls.
In winters, we decorated
our flower vases
with chrysanthemums the color
of tiny pink cakes.
In summers our fathers
took us to drink
green mango sorbet
at the same quaint little joint.
Springs and autumns were
the times for new clothes
during festivals as even trees
turned fashion-conscious
and flaunted their dresses.

Strange that we never met as kids—
not in this life, anyway.
I wonder if I have known you
in other lives before in kindergarten,
when you were my favorite playmate.
Perhaps we decorated chrysanthemums
together in one flower vase.

EROS THANATOS

1

Tiny blue and green stars
are beads on my face on the body
that prowls the horizons of
sweet pudding, or jelly love.
Bright mauves on lower eyelids
play footsie with the
golden lads and lasses.
A black lace choker with
a dark green rose
chokes my floating neck
killing the voice, so the bartender
howls to the moon.

2

I don't pray I will go to hell
for sure I drank coconut and cherries
as bartender howled at concoctions
and the Moon covered her split ears
and tall dusky women wanted me in bed
while I prowl for the men sliding off
my back and running off with my choker
with now-torn green rose

so that I can scream blue murder most foul...
but the tall women stop my mouth
dragging me to bed while
the jealous bartender grows two Dali heads
and the Moon wears my pilfered choker
scolding me for past and present tense
while the women's flickering tongues
pillage my stars smudge the colors
blue green mauve

HOW I WANT YOU GREEN
(with thanks to Frederico Garcia Lorca)

How I want you green!

(Because I am not green
I am
a bit of silver
a brimful of blue)

I want you in
a hundred shades
of emerald and jade
the hue of gooseberries
and tender stalks

My roses of yesterday
you wrap in velvet green
I float on waters
near moss-green rocks

How I want you green!
Do you know now?
Do you know how?
Have you seen?
Have you seen?
Have you read the words
in between?

ASPEN

The bottle of Aspen perfume you sent for me
remained for two decades in my wardrobe.
Aspen is not sweet:
my friends claimed it smelled of whiskey,
and I always sprinkled some onto my
dyed *bandhini* dupattas, which I seldom washed.
Perhaps everyone suspected that I was drunk
every time I donned a dupatta, especially
your favorite crushed cerulean
with lace detailing and white polka dots.
Perhaps it was not just sartorial:
it could have been my dreamy
eighteen-year old eyes hiding the memory
of your first proposal,
which always made me blush.

Today I blush at how I rejected you
for poetry.
Tonight, as on every night,
I sleep with books piled
on my bed,
nobody by my side.

PORCELAIN
(with thanks to Mallika Bhaumik)

My dad always bought me
porcelain coffee mugs.
The latest is dainty white
with pale pink roses
and grey leaves on the outside.
I escape pain with chai latte
at the first ray of light.

I remember, too, teacups
from long ago —
one brick-orange and
another teal-blue.
We exchanged the cups
every day by turn, and
so, we had no fights
under the sun.

The last you gave me
was a mug with hearts
like a teenager's restless trust.
And yet, one day
you left us behind, and we
gathered dust.

FLIES

it is cold enough
to break stones
in the mound of flesh
lodged in my rib cage

you scooped out
the insides
like the sweet yellow part
of a lemon tart
and left the crust for flies

(and who wants
to buy a bitten peach?
or feel nauseated
if asked to eat?)

only the flies
neglect the difference
between truth and lies

TO AP: HOW TO FALL IN LOVE AGAIN

First, think of Langston Hughes
and his Eve whose eyes
were a bit too bold—
then, look into my eyes
to catch the flash of quickening desire.
Third step is to dream up perfection
(or, you can even adorn each imperfection
with a flower).
Fourth, you need to think again:
what if you actually touched a color-emitting disco-ball
or a star shimmering hot?
Next—is to touch—
let your index finger caress
a soft cheek, or let
our lips speak in whispers,
pressed together, striving for fire.
Sixth is to obliterate the many pasts,
and kiss as if this love will be
your last.

BLACK ZONES
(For Mallika Bhaumik)

1

The fragrance of black tea
and incense on a
winter evening without love
is a quiet drug.

Distraction is whether
it is time to wash the
old but perfectly good
multicolored woolen sweater
with red buttons intact.

Comfort is your friend's
book of poems that echoes
your melancholia and gives you
something to clutch and
feel tangible feelings.

A slice of seasonal fruit cake
stops you from fainting with hunger.

2

The sky is still blue.
The grass is still green.
The rose is still red.

Van Gogh's sunflowers are your
soul's antithesis.

On starry nights, you leave out
the stars and paint only
the black zones of the universe.

Love leaves you like starlight
through your fingers.

SUFI IN THE GARDEN
(For Sufia Khatoon)

1

There's a Sufi in the garden of falling jasmines.
I spread a silk scarf in the rain
to catch the flowers and listen
to her paradise-verse.

She sings of walking on stars
of orange summers and ripe mangoes
of death in the holy month
and of life and hope

2

I am lost in the wet garden
and don't want to be found

I feel the night in Sufi's
jasmine-washed hair

as she treads with her songs
from star to star

AS OLD AS ME
(For Nikita Parik)

When you are as old as me,
you bite into Grief as if
it is a Shrewsbury biscuit
from your favorite Colaba shop.
Disappointment tastes like black grapes
you savor on your palate;
you admire the purple stain
on your tongue.
These harsh consonants are
on the standard Atlas of the route—
the little key on the side
gives it all away.
I don't remember if they are
bilabial or labio-dental or
any other analysis down the
dusty bookshelves of my
phonetics textbook.

I only know the flavors, too familiar
when you are as old as me...

with the softened edges of
vocabulary, you know that
Pain is the blue zone of the map...
the three-fourths part, the sea.

SOAP CAKE

I was four
and remember my first taste
of ice cream – strawberry-flavored
in a small paper cup sold at
our local park, as a treat from
my father. This was sunset.
Next morning, he took me for a walk
and, after I had played with the soil for a while
introduced me to the jasmine tree
in the wildly flourishing garden.
He lifted me up
so that I can pick some jasmines.
My mother scolded me for dirty hands,
and for a long time, my palms
smelled of jasmines and forgotten soap cake.

After more than thirty years,
I try tons of soap cakes
and smell them
like one addicted, so that
I can pick jasmines again.

UNDUSTED

Thick layers of sorrow remain undusted
in the corners of my bookcase;
a journal with a *Daphnis and Chloe* cover
is trapped in the messy inner passages
that don't exist on paper maps.
A cream-hued rose is squeezed
between the covers.
My body barely squeezes itself
between ancient structures stained
with a hundred years of neglect.

I open a heavy wooden drawer
to discover tidy rows of Science textbooks
left behind by a grandfather;
a page falls open to diagrams
of funnels and test tubes.
For a moment, I am perplexed
as to why Sulphur is yellow.
I then wonder how brass and copper
are different: perhaps the same way
as loneliness and desolation are, and
being left out of spheres is.

I discover an empty little vintage tin
of sour mints and put
three watercolor cakes inside
to paint, later on, sulphuric flowers
under cobalt skies imprisoning
an alkaline, litmus-paper sun.
Today my forgotten journal smells like a rose.

FLOWER PATTERNS

1
She kept wildflowers
in a white teacup
filled with water

The pink chintz curtains,
floral-patterned, were sewn
by her own hand

She embroidered blue pansies
on my handkerchief, now
too precious for Indian summers

The wallpaper was designed
with blue and yellow flowers
brightening the room

2
She lived with flowers
fresh in the teacup

She died with flowers
still fresh, in the teacup

DALI AND THE COFFEE HOUSE*

1

At the west side of the
isle of the dead
a couple with their
heads full of clouds
played out the coffee house
scene in Madrid.
The waiter, a soft monster,
brought them fried egg
on the plate without the plate
and two pieces of bread.

2

He stood across the street
from the cathedral of thumbs
and drew a self-portrait
of the artist in studio,
listening to the invisible harp.
*I think honey is sweeter
than blood*, he conceded,
expressing the sentiment of love.

*The lines of the poem are taken from titles of paintings by
Salvador Dali

THE SECOND WALTZ: A RESPONSE*

Whether I dream
of being in a ballroom
wearing a yellow silk dress
or, whether I lose myself
in a garden of damask roses
and sea-green butterflies–
the Second Waltz weaves
a cocoon between
insanity and I.
The surreal infuses itself
into the real
like a little bag of
comforting mint tea
drunk with a slow intake
of sighs on lonely evenings.
When thoughts of giving up
become vines around the soul,
Shostakovich untangles me
in response.

The music loosens a chignon
down to the waist
so that I
rush out to the garden
and re-do my hair
with a pastel butterfly.

*The Second Waltz is a musical composition by Dmitri
Shostakovich.

STORM*

What's in a storm?
Vivaldi, it brews
in the skies
inside
amidst
the symphony of
winds pregnant
with the Furies
of the heart

I stand, unafraid
in the gale,
arms outstretched
listening to you as
the flying dust
surrounds me
revolves around me
spins like a record player
on a gramophone

I drown, Vivaldi,
in the storm
stubborn, alone

*Refers to the musical composition 'Storm' by Antonio
Vivaldi, a part of his Seasons (Summer)

CARNIVAL

1

The dead cannot feel the sun in their skulls
like I do, dazed at the carnival of bodies.
Men and women lie next to one another
adorned in their best attire—and flowers.
The incense in the air is a drug
in the October fest at Keoratola.*
The sounds of wailing reach a
near-operatic crescendo.

I wonder if the permanently sleeping,
stirred by the music, will get up and dance.
After all, dancing is the vertical expression
of a horizontal desire.
Now, it is not a sin to sleep with strangers.

2

I have witnessed many a beloved
go into their communal baths of fire;
even touched their chests and helped them enter.
I remember smoke wafting from their limbs.

Dry-eyed, I dream of them and still
repeat conversations to myself,
whispered in the night.

I also wonder who will sleep with me
when I join the carnival.

*A crematorium in Kolkata

FOR MARY LAMB

P.S. - I have known since last year that I am going crazy.

1

Monastery or mental asylum—
which of them will provide me
a feast of sugar plums?

My hollowed body is possessed
by Van Gogh and Mary Lamb—
sunflowers and Shakespeare in my brain.
Is there a mind?
Something leaches out of me
into a dank-smelling drain on
the fast *bahn*, a German train.
The Elbe and the Rhine
flow through my head.

2

At Schloss Pilnitz I witnessed
a production of King Lear—
oh, what a falling off was there!
There was real thunder and rain.
I don't remember the end,
but the audience screamed when

Regan plucked out Gloucester's eyes
and blood ran down her arms
and I laughed and laughed
because I knew it was all lies.

3
I pluck out memories to prove I am not dead.
I am both mad Lear and blind Gloucester who bled.
The lunatic, the lover, and the poet live in a
midsummer shed.
Van Gogh's bullet is lodged in my head.

COLD BLUE: ON D. G. ROSSETTI'S
PROSERPINE

Cold blue my eyes,
cold with sorrow,
and cold blue the drapes
of my silk dress in winter...
the smoky lamp my only light.

How many of my kind
have shared my plight?
Six months away from
my beloved world, I live
in Hades, Pluto's captive.
The Dark God's strength
has been my prison,
and Jupiter's decree
sealed my fate.
He says my lips are red
like the wild abandon of this
fiery pomegranate I hold—
my treason, I was told,
is that I ate six seeds
offered (to a hungry goddess)
in Hades.

I lie beside a god
I love not—I cool his lust
on every wintry underworld
night...

How many, still, fall like me?
How many, still, share my plight?

GODDESS
(after Margaret Atwood)

You think I am not a goddess?
Wet and salty my skin...
far from a peach.
My years have rolled out
of your reach.
To you, I will give
an orange cotton scarf
scented with jasmine.
You'll know my youth then—
how the fruit was sweet
and flowers perfumed.
Mind you, I won't allow
the bones to be exhumed—
a scarf is all you get.

You think I am not a goddess yet?
Think again—I am every woman
with a hidden palimpsest of scars
like tattoos covering every inch
of where it hurts.
Call me—yes! —call me anything,
by any name! Only remember...
I am a goddess still.
I will not be tamed.

SELF-PORTRAIT AS NYX*

1

I walk in the ether-scented intoxication
of lonely power
past the planet-gods who watch in awe.
Stars wash my hair and the firmament
is my body.
I dress in muslin clouds.

2

It is not easy to be born
out of Chaos;
nor to give birth to Thanatos.
My son Hypnos exists behind eyelids,
and Hemera, my beautiful child, follows
me at work — my dichotomy, my binary.

3

The God of Thunder turns away in fear—
he loves women who submit.
Leda and Europa are to his taste:
I am not.
My fiery soul has no answering echo—
I wear shimmering moon-fragments
on my bosom to murder hunger.

*Goddess of Night in Greek mythology

'THE BEAUTY HAS COME': NEFERTITI*

They say, with time beauty dies.
All lies.

I am known only for a beautiful face.
They remark on my lotus eyes, perfect chin,
scarlet lips, exotic headgear and necklace inlaid.
That's all—there's no more to tell—
for I ruled Egypt, and ruled it well.
With my husband Akhenaten, I remained—
no Caesar, no Antony till the end.

A plague took my life, not an asp.
A life well-lived is out of the grasp
of Drama and Art.
No actor clamors to play my part.

For eons, I'm a gorgeous bust:
no woman's envy, no man's lust
no historian's delight
no scholar's pride

I stand for you to see
what happens when history
is forgotten, and you are
a non-entity—
Nothing great, nothing remarkable.
Only a powerful queen who did not fall.
It's nothing apparently.
Nothing at all.

*Bust of Nefertiti viewed by me at Egyptian Museum,
Berlin in 2005

CANESCENT

1
These mornings, I wake to find
silver threads in my hair—
gleaming as if dipped
in the winter moon.

I have always loved
oxidized ornaments and grey pullovers;
but now, afraid of canescent
I fantasize about a smooth cinnamon coverage.

I tell my dad: let me get highlights.
And so on I press.
(No, this looks beautiful, Dad says.)

2
(Dad asks: Do you want your strands to be
stained
bright-red like betel juice?)

My imagination turns loose.

I ponder into a salt-seasoned mulberry fruit.
I conjure up watery chiaroscuro skies
of the collective unconscious.
The silkworm, an outsider, would have preferred a
mulberry leaf.

I realize I live under ancient oaks.
My hair has the shade of experience now, I guess.

(*Yes, it does, and this looks lovely*: Dad says).

GRIEF

1

What do you do when you grieve?
All I do is explode; inside
an inferno chars the house
and a violet is deflowered.
My imagery jars in alleys blind
where pain bangs on doors, entry denied.
It is black and cold and smells of damp ash.

2

I grieve because I am lost
and have no rationality left;
feverish, I dream of you as a lover
and long to secure you in a clutch.
My bipolar brain sinks in the horizon
splashed with the color of the
tart lava of moon cycles flowing down my legs;
glowing to pull in and drown you;
now wild, unmated...
like Lear my throat explodes in a howl.*

*from Act 5 Scene 3 of King Lear, a tragic play by
Shakespeare

FADING

Incredulous
at the fading
of your signatures
from a deep crimson to a pale peach
to a blank space...

I load
a brown paper bag to its mouth
with nectarines and peaches...

I hoard sweetness
with grief-fueled bites
but soon, the brown paper bag lies
empty on my bed, sans a caress...

ON FINDING MY OLD POETRY
NOTEBOOK

Speaking to myself, twenty years ago
I sketched pine trees.
Needles dripped with dew and
the cones were hard and cold.
Winters were blue and white
and green and brown.
The sound was of water dripping
from branches stretching
towards me and away from me.
The rain formed a fountain
over the shivering moon
amidst the icicles of stars.

I have re-discovered
a teenager's
solitary dreamlike noon
of off-seasonal poems...

I re-invent the winter
in dark brittle ink

ON NOT FINDING AN OLDER
POETRY NOTEBOOK

It had a teal, marble-finish hardcover.

Every afternoon, after school hours
its A6 pages absorbed my sighs
over George Harrison and his gently weeping guitar.
Bombay has no winter, and the mild
November wind blowing from the Arabian Sea
through my bedroom window was
the perfect accompaniment to
The Beatles' songs or Harrison's solos
that played as I composed my own lines, fancying myself
either a 1990s Anne Frank or Shelley the rebel...
all of thirteen.
I was not sure about God, but George
was My Sweet Lord and I really wanted to see him...

I have forgotten the titles of my poems
except one—"Colors From My Guitar"—
where I imagined a candlelit evening
in Liverpool, where I'd never be...

AGONY

The veiled sculpture that Ali
creates of Maryam in
Dokhtar Irooni has come back
to haunt me after ten years...

Each word I write for you
is a block of marble—each sentence
an imperfect sculpture of the infatuation
that is you...

I wish my fingers could chisel you
out of the intricate design of every rose,
from each piece of terracotta and jeweled lacquer
in both prose and verse...

(Since I cannot speak your name)

I long to
sew you into a green velvet leaf
plant you in the center of stars
compose you in a sonata
carry you in the dark like a lantern...

All the while burning, burning, burning
in the agony of the sculptor
dumb with desire

Ref: Dokhtar Irooni (Persian Girl) is an Iranian movie
released in 2003.

THE AUTUMNAL

The apogee of a baroque passion
is wetness... but the rest of the body
is draped in autumnal layers of
tan dress, black jacket, black leggings, tan boots–
tan and black feel as soft as
the outer consciousness veiling
ornate nakedness dyed in sunset resplendence
seen only in wet eyes and heavy breathing...

rubbing a rose on nude lips
to conjure you and rescind
the touch of the shameful flesh
of past lives. Wild salty lips can dream
of flowers...

the body awakens, abjures dreams, and undresses...
black and tan strewn on the autumnal lawn;
now, only the gorgeous look and feel of
womanhood in love —

wet wet wet

MAHTAB

1
You named her Mahtab nine years ago–
I wonder if Mahtab is dead today.

(The version before Mahtab loved Eliot.
She wanted to be the Hyacinth Girl,
with wet eyes and hair.)

Mahtab's words were bubbles against the sky.
"Jor ba khair, jaan jora?"
were the calligraphy of her lips.

(For you, she painted her lips scarlet.
For you, she wore lavender in bed.)

Was she the one you called azizam?
Was she the one who said, "Doostet daram"?

For you, Mahtab dreamt of moon and stars
For you, Mahtab wore a Prussian blue scarf
For you, Mahtab cooked meat in tomato paste
For you, phrases of love rolled off her tongue

azizam
doostet daram
dibunatam

Well, Eshgeman, I still wonder if Mahtab is dead.

2
I now recall the soprano sound
of love shattering like a crystal glass
as Mahtab drank oceans of her own passion.
I seem to remember all of a sudden
that Mahtab kept drinking oceans of salty tears
till she drowned.

(At the time of death,
she wore lavender, loved hyacinth poetry,
and her hair was wet.)

azizam
dibunatam
doostet daram

Eshgeman, now I know Mahtab is dead.

Mahtab was too thirsty
Mahtab drank an ocean too many

Noshjaan

Glossary (Farsi/Dari)

Jor ba khair/jan jora – How are you? Is everything fine?
Azizam - sweetheart
Dibunatam - crazy for you
Doostet daram - I love you
Eshgeman - my love
Noshjan - may your soul be satisfied
(usually said to a person who is about to eat or drink)
Mahtab - moonlight

ASSIGNATION

You wanted an assignation
and kept messaging me for place and time.
I was making myself a cup of tea
to relieve a sore body.
You were enquiring about a hotel room
with bathtub where you could
scratch poems on my skin.
I was busy pouring hot water
from the hissing electric kettle.
You thought I wasn't paying attention:
it was not true.
I was trying to, but my bodyache was killing me
and the scent of lemon-ginger tea
in a Red Rose teabag was maddening.
The black cat asked me for food in the
language of her tribe.
I took a warm sip from my cup
and thought it was the perfect time to
reply to you.
Then I saw the cat eating the yellow dahlias
from the precious white vase.
I hastened to scold her and give her treats.
I managed to save the dahlias,
but by then, it was too late for you.

PRESTO AGITATO

I think of the night
you shared with me
the third movement of the
Moonlight Sonata*.
Today, your piano silences me
in my grief of losing you.
I crave for a violin
for relief to seek Vivaldi.
My Storm**, your Presto Agitato***...

I can touch turmoil in the skies
thunder in the mountains
wild rain in my eyes
lightning that strikes the window pane..
I have lost you in the storm.
The lightning strikes again
the moon catches fire
goes up in flames
in thunder and rain...

I am a madwoman
lost in the storm

from hair to toe
presto agitato
thunder and rain
How do I translate losing you?
How do I translate the tongue
of pain?

*Composition by Beethoven
**Composition by Vivaldi
***The third movement of the Moonlight Sonata

WILLOW
(with thanks to Amit Shankar Saha)

1
I am a willow. He loves the birch.

2
Only the sad moist soil
holds me fast.
I weep to make
legends come true.

In cool summers, he looks away
from my blue-green lush.
In frozen winters, the snow
in a pious rush, covers
my naked deciduous form.

Born in temperate season,
my Being is a tropical storm.
I weep in a hush.

3
I offer him a single blue leaf–
an oval mirror
teardrop stained.

He asks me if it has rained.
He hastens to save the birch.

MAPS
(for Amit Shankar Saha)

1
If
the maps of our being
are preordained

then
I am a part
of
your subcontinent

(lands touch
and oceans merge)

That is why
there is something similar
in our poems, I tell you,
as if like siblings
they have a family resemblance...

You and I write about trees—
you hug a birch,
I discover a willow within

growing on the plateau
of friendship

2
I make a holy bonfire
of wet Fall leaves
and offer you the smoke,
fragrant, suspended,
like a screen

only for the sake
of watching you
spend winters
sharing silverfish
with the goddess
of our subcontinent

WILLOW 2
(with thanks to Amit Shankar Saha)

Some winters are so cold
that I discover a willow within.

You write poems on the birch.
I am a weeping willow
with a shivering blue heart.
I'm your Deirdre of the Sorrows[*]
by the river down which
Ophelia[**] floated in a white dress.
Did you hear her dying song?
Winter's leaves are wet with
yesterday's rain.

This December nineteen
I look beyond the river
and watch you
build the Pacific Ocean.

You look up only to tell me:
sadness suits the poet. Be thankful.

[*]Deirdre of the Sorrows is from Irish folklore
[**]Ophelia is from Shakespeare's Hamlet

FISH
(In response to Amit Shankar Saha)

To mingle your breath with mine
I come bearing dreams of the Rhine.
Of thirteen years ago a tale–
you bent the time and I set sail.
Today I am your guest,
and you offer me food and rest—
a fish and a leaf that she had sent...
to me you served, generously spent.
We breathe the same atoms free
as I brew up a lazy tea.
To mask the smell of fish I consume
curiously strong breath mints, and assume
that when you give me a fish–
it is your version of a kiss.

ALONE
(dedicated to Linda Ashok)

Being alone is good
if you don't wear black
with sequins

and plain and bare
you lay your head
on your copy
of Shelley
(crinkled with age because
it belonged to your grandpa)...

you don't pull off a satin dress
with sequins well;
and by now
you have forgotten
how to sew on
those large yellow buttons
on white floral cotton

RAINDROP

I dream that
*raindrops keep falling
on my head.*[*]
(My parched earth
cracked on the crust
begs to be wet).

I dream I were
soaked in the rain.
(Fruitless humidity
makes my dress
cling to my shoulders
like a stubborn fragrance).

I long to write a poem
without you on my mind.
But you are like the raindrop
of my dreams.

*title of a song by BJ Thomas

STONE

I'm your blue-stone
turquoise woman—

green-blue
sky-blue...

The turquoise woman
you wore in your
silver ring...

The turquoise woman
of decadent springs

who to you clings
as the bird's claw
clutches the sky

as ripeness fills all berries

as the sun in the west
does lie...

With your every breath
you hear me sigh...

I'm your turquoise woman
to cherish
when the fermented rice wine
makes me cry

SEASONAL
(Based on Shakespeare's Sonnets 98 and 109)

It is the winter of your separation
in the summer of April, even though
the hot rose smells of you

The bleak branches grow
into the cold veins under
my skin, and I cannot hear
the birds sing

(You have been absent all spring)

No flings for me to fill
the time, yet I
carry water to wash the stain
of absence

I carry water
to wash, fruitlessly,
the inked patterns of sorrow

I call you the rose
and you my all

No wonder, then, that
summer is actually winter
and I played with your shadows
all season

SUMMER DAYS

In summers, the sun always enters my eyes
and caresses my forehead like
a bunch of bright feathers.
My mother and I greedily consume
orange ice cream sticks,
ignoring my weight issues.
Other times, April is a
frothy sweet green sherbet
that my father treats me to.
The neighborhood wakes and sleeps
to the scented lull of mangoes and jasmines.
I doze in the drowsy afternoons,
dreaming of paper-thin bougainvillea
that adorned my childhood terrace.
The heat penetrates my sunblock cream.
My skin turns into a salty tamarind,
which I wash with splashing water while
listening to warbling finches, wrens, sparrows
discussing the weather in the garden.
I can hear the roses in pink muslin and taffeta
planning an exclusive party.
I think I asked their damask leader:
is this the pinnacle of pleasure?

UNSPOKEN

Your razor blade
cuts into my finger-mounds.
I bleed unspoken words
onto every virgin page.

Red blue green violet
to soak and sink
our teeth of rage—

here and there
the paper tears
like the end-rhymes
of a senseless pledge.

The ends of my hands
bleed words till white
and dry swells my sight...

dare you remember this image?

LABYRINTH

I can only feel depression as a cold labyrinth.
It is dark and I am afraid of even
a single star sharing its light.
I must have collided with an iceberg
and am sinking like the Titanic.
The Atlantic is deeper than I saw
in my dreams.

It is the land of perpetual winter
where snow is not pretty anymore.
My liquid blood has crystallized
and there is now pale ice
frozen in my veins.
All I can do is cling to my bed
unable to rise.

My mind is a sunless labyrinth
where sorrows awake.
I sew together
the corpses of the past
and preserve them in the enameled
coffin made of ice. I write poems
to stifle the cries.

BREAKFAST

I breathe in pale-orange mornings
while sweeping the driveway—
my broomstick swishing the leaves
into a golden hill.
I brew pumpkin-spice coffee
in memory of a three-year old autumn.
Water gurgles as two eggs
boil in a sleek red pan.
The white toaster noisily evicts
two crisp pieces of brown toast.

And yet,
when I serve you breakfast
on the balcony from which
you can clearly see the tidied driveway...
you complain of my Silence.

I sit with a coloring book for adults
running lemon and pink crayons
meticulously over illustrated flowers
as
dreams of buying a blender
and making myself a banana smoothie
visit me frequently enough to become
a New Year's resolution.

LOSING

In Bhawanipur, stands a house
green like a Jim Carey mask.
It is new paint. When I first opened
my eyes to the world, it had been
an old, cracked yellow.

I knew not better than
dark red floors, tacky pink walls, and leaf-green doors
(populated by gloomy furniture).
The only ornate piece was
my great-grandfather's glossy, wooden, black bookcase.
It had large dragons carved on the panels.

(I took out a forbidden book from there
named *Anna Karenina* and read it at eleven...
but that's a later story).

Another story of later years is
how I traveled to different cities
all over the world searching for the
semblance of red floors, pink walls, and green doors.
I could not buy my first consciousness back.
Nor I found a love that promised me this semblance.
(My cousin inherited the wooden bookcase and broke
the dragons, and I cannot find my copy of *Anna
Karenina*.)

SOULS

My mother has the gift of pairing up
my long-separated socks.
God knows how she finds them!

She seems to believe in Plato's concept of souls,
and many socks have rediscovered their mates
under her aegis.
For instance,
a lonely gooseberry-green summer beauty,
sleeping in the Godrej *almirah*, would be reunited
with its twin-soul which was in a plastic basket in
another story.

After the remarriage of as many true pairs
as she could find, mother
would keep them in a pink satin bag,
proudly showing me its contents of
cotton, net, nylon, and wool,
bought from Chinese shops
and roadside stalls.
I had a penchant for colors and flowers
and strawberries and various impractical designs.
These now nestled together, each with its

perfect match, in the satin bag.
I felt the thrill of recognition.
They were pliant in my hands, rendering me
the monarch of all I surveyed.

I then ventured to compliment mom
on her grand success as a sock-cupid.
She smiled, and said, "Ah! But I could not find
a match for you. I feel my work is incomplete."

I remember pouring my heart and soul into
choosing the right pair for work the next day.

TAH-DIG

1

I still cook rice in open pots,
letting the fragrance that you loved
stray through the wind.
You preferred my white rice
to your Persian *tah-dig*,
(which
I, an adept cook, adorned for you
with red sour *zereshk* berries,
while we bit into the crisp oil-fried layer
at the bottom like a cake).

2

I went last year
to the best Parsee restaurant in Mumbai,
Mother and Father in tow.
I was startled to see *tah-dig*
on the table after ten long years.
"This is delicious," my parents exclaimed.

I remained silent, not telling them
that they had just paid Rs 700

for a dish that their daughter
could cook way better at home.

Except, it is not the same home
that I shared with you.

Glossary:
> *Tah-dig*: Rice cooked in Persian style
> *Zereshk*: Dried barberry fruit

LIME GREEN LEAF

Lime green leaf
(was it tender?)
I gave you one
and you left it
neglected it,
then autumn came
too soon

Crisp golden leaves
are pretty
but they disintegrate
when you try
to paste them
in your record book
of loves

REMAKING MAGIC CARPET
AND FINDING PINK SNEAKERS
(with thanks to Lynda Hull)

Please lend me your magic carpet,
or let me sit beside you for a while.
To cramp your style is not my goal,
but the new wool is now old;
the best wool of Garment District is now fraying.
I have brought my own yarn.
I will remake your carpet with black and gold.
I don't like the white, for white is always graying.

Why do I need your carpet?
Why can I not run?
Because I lost my pink sneakers in the Past,
and my memory is sore with me.
I have looked at the shelves of every city store
but found none
And so, I need your carpet to run
in the hour of the sun when the
Moon is full and in Capricorn.
Only then can the carpet become
a glowworm in the dark, or a lantern.

Let the Past swirl by like a footloose cloud;
but I imagine it will spew out
my pink sneakers like a star.
I need the magic carpet to show off
so that the crowd from my Past
does not blacken and tar me
for being too wild and free.
You understand now that
the only things I need
are gold and black wool, and speed.

COATS

I've never seen my mom's doctor uncle
who wore the coats hanging
in his wife's wardrobe.
They were of the eclectic colors
that gentlemen were fond of
—tan grey silver black,
each of them bought on separate trips to England.
Next to the wardrobe was a wooden dresser too,
with drawers crammed with his medical books,
all remnants of his life as a student in London.

My grandma kept pink jars of cold cream
atop the dresser, along with
a vintage lemon-yellow powder box
that was filled with lavender talc.
She generously let me use the cosmetics
but never allowed me to touch the coats.

Grandma lived for thirty years in a world
without her husband.
Now that she is gone, I still think
about the coats.

SKIN

I have the satiny skin
of a wayward peach
bursting with desire for sin
running in my veins
barely covered by satin and georgette

the silence within
my erstwhile cloister
is harder to break;
though the eyes seem eager,
thirsts are harder to slake

I send for you a transparent packet
of potpourri I own

I've lost my voice, and dried flowers
understand skin tones

TARFIA ON BEAUTY
(Based on a conversation over breakfast with poet *Tarfia Faizullah* at Bear River Writers' Conference, 2018)

If I had raw-silk hair
and sapphire eyes,
and shod myself in green satin

If my face launched
red lipsticks and black limousines

If, five hundred years ago,
I was Botticelli's creation

If I could immortalize Faustus
with a kiss to his damnation

Then, Tarfia,
I wouldn't have complained
in the morning rain
that I am not beautiful
and you would not have joined
me at breakfast
only to tell:
"I will fight with you

if you ever say again
that you are not beautiful."

Tarfia, you often wore
lavender eyeshadow—
pearlescent, with a sheen

Tarfia,
lavender would not
have been so beautiful
if you had not been

TASBIH

I never used the *janamaz*
nor finished the bottle
of deep green *jannat-al-firdaus*.
The purple velvet bag
from Kabul Shopping Center with
colorful pastel leaves was a tad
too gorgeous for my classes.
You were the fantasy of every girl
who was plain and wore glasses.

If I hear the *azaan* nowadays,
it is by accident:
I try not to make out the words
that I once knew by heart.
I try not to think of Surah Kausar
and the ambrosia denied to me
when I lost my paradise.
I never tell people I learnt
to love strong liquor tea from you,
sometimes sucking on
a candy or a sugar cube.
I have kept your blue *tasbih*

in my jewelry box:
my mother thinks
it is a necklace.

GLOSSARY

Janamaz– Muslim prayer rug
Jannat-al-Firdaus– a popular perfume
Azaan– call to prayer
Surah Kausar– The 108th and shortest chapter of the *Quran*
Tasbih– prayer beads

A TECHNICAL WRITER TRIES TO FORGET

1
I do not have
bandwidth

to touch your
cosmos
netted with stars

and must un-press
the keys that
installed you
in the portals
of my soul

2
Writing-architectures
make me
trace
your shape

(Insert Image)

my frantic desperation
changes the symphony
of commands

(Delete Image)

3
My system click-opens
poems of loss

I extract pages
and save them
to the empty folder
of the aching heart

THE METAPOEM

My poems are vinyl dolls
that I make for you
sketching in eyes and nose and lips
with watercolor ink.

My poems are glass lanterns—
every time one is lit on nights
when the soul has no electricity
from within.

My poems are perfumes of opium
to fog my brain with restfulness,
and flavors of marijuana to keep me high.
Or perhaps, they are shining moons
that children cut out of
gold and silver paper from
classic cigarette boxes.

My poems are the proof that I am breathing.
My poems are a dusty tempest seething.
Each a life. Some despair. Some glee.
A volcano. A waterfall. A placid lake. A tree.
Image upon image of wild birds grateful to be free.

TWILIGHT

Twilight's stars are the coolest eyedrops.
I recover my sight to exercise
the debatable right
of bestowing on you my gaze.

The evening bell tolls from the temple;
I imagine sacred flames on holy lamps—
as always, I wonder if it is a sin
to surrender and to the ground
my ego raze.

The night is a soft flower on my mouth;
supple petals, firm taste — abandoned
by an earthly lover, I am blind.
I cannot rest.

MEMENTO MORI*

Memento mori

I cannot forget
the dead
nor that one day
you will count me
in their rank and file

Memento mori

so what if you
loved not me?
The obliteration of memory
will happen too—
same for me, same for
the immortal queen of the Nile

Memento mori

what is lost and
what is gained?
Yesterday was sun
and today it rained...
when the candle flickers out
do not doubt
we'd have loved a while

*Remember thou art mortal

SELF OBITUARY

Her life was a filigree-work
of several loves
all entwined in her essence.
Turquoise pain, too,
mingled in her being
with crimson grief.

She lived. She breathed
the same atom as you.
Her eyes widened at
sun-yellow hopes too.

She was soft. She cried
over lost loves and
sought refuge in
a poet's purple loft.

She found comfort
in a blank page,
soothing herself with
silk-black ink.

After she was consumed
on her pyre,
a plain urn contained
her ashes of desire.
Her being mingled with
the Arabian Sea:
she rested now
to her heart's content.
The waves submerged her fire.

www.ingramcontent.com/pod-product-compliance
Lightning Source LLC
Chambersburg PA
CBHW021936040426
42448CB00008B/1089